Serenity Swirls

A CALMING COLORING BOOK

BY JENNIFER LANKENAU

DIVERSIONBOOKS

Diversion Books
A Division of Diversion Publishing Corp.
443 Park Avenue South, Suite 1008
New York, New York 10016
www.DiversionBooks.com

For more information, email info@diversionbooks.com

First Diversion Books edition September 2015.
Print ISBN: 978-1-68230-183-8

Printed in the USA
CPSIA information can be obtained
at www.ICGtesting.com
JSHW072027140824
68134JS00042B/3812

9 781682 301838